FEAR THE NINJA

Demystifying Cryptocurrency Trading

An intermediate guide to trading with crypto coins

Volume 2

George Samaris

Table of Contents

Introduction

Here we are, getting ready to take on another cryptocurrency journey because the concept of digital currencies doesn't end with just one book or idea. Whatever you know about cryptocurrency is just a foundation; there are layers to this concept that have to be unravelled, and that is the purpose of this book, to help you learn all about cryptocurrencies from an advanced perspective. This book was put together for individuals who have started with cryptos but need to upgrade their knowledge.

Now, if you don't know anything or know so much about cryptocurrency and you are reading this material, you may want to get my book *Cryptocurrency World*, it is a definitive guide on everything a beginner should know about crypto coins. We continue with vast ideas on how you can get the most out of the digital currency in the world today.

If you have been trading with cryptocurrencies before now, you will come across some familiar terms, and you will also discover very new words that show the extent of growth that the sector has recorded within a few years. If you want to get the most out of this book; as you read, make up your mind that you are going to implement everything you learn. Even though we are taking on an advanced course, the principles of cryptocurrencies are pretty much the same; you must use your money to prove that you are willing to jump right in.

Cryptocurrencies are now a part of our financial system, trust me when I say it isn't going anywhere anytime soon. As such, you have a responsibility to learn as much as you can. The most successful crypto investors never take a break from learning, we are going to learn more about why we are making an advanced lesson in the very first chapter, but until then, you should know that even after reading this book, your quest for more knowledge on the subject shouldn't end.

Open your mind to learn, to grow and to become much more innovative with everything that pertains to cryptocurrencies. The investor who updates his knowledge will always have the edge over the one who doesn't. So you need to ask yourself what kind of investor do you want to be; the former or the latter?

Our first chapter begins in earnest as we get to learn why we should take on an advanced lesson. An understanding of the "Why" will lead us to know the "How," flip over and enjoy the read.

Chapter One

Advanced Cryptocurrency; why go further?

You probably already know all about Bitcoin, trading platforms, ICOs, etc., so here you are with a book that promises to take things up a notch with advanced crypto knowledge and you are wondering, why. Before we get right to the main sections of this book, I want to use this opportunity to share some insight on why we are taking on this journey. At the end of this chapter, you will be inspired to learn more as knowledge is never-ending.

Most people wander through life mostly because they are not AWARE of what they are supposed to be doing here. There is the need for awareness on why we do the things we do; why did you buy this book? Why are you reading through it now? You see for everything we decide to do; we must ask the necessary questions else the purpose of what we do will be lost. So here, we are asking, why is it essential for us to go further with an advanced cryptocurrency book? You will find the answers below;

Why we learn advanced cryptocurrency

1. The world is moving at a fast pace

One of the primary reasons why you should learn about cryptocurrencies from a sophisticated perspective is because the world is moving at a breakneck speed as such it is crucial that you run at the same level else you will be left behind. Some investors do not make the right choices as time goes by because they are limited by knowledge. Get to know more, and you will gain insight into how you can be better on your cryptocurrency journey.

2. It is the future

Cryptocurrencies are the future!

Crypto coins is shaping the concept of digital finance, and it isn't about to stop soon. Whatever you read today, whatever you add to your wealth of knowledge will be extremely useful to you in the future. Now is the time to gather information as you can and then utilize them to your advantage.

3.   We have invested in it

When you invest in something (no matter how small), you should also be interested in how that thing or concept turns out. With cryptocurrencies, you use the money to buy into the system and then expect returns in the form of money as well. So you should be interested in how the venture spans out; don't sit still waiting for a weekly or monthly subscribed newsletter from a crypto firm (though this is also important)

Anything that has to do with money must be taken seriously, and the best way to discover if your investment is safe with promised yields is by reading and learning more about the way investment works.

4.   New ideas are introduced often

Advanced lessons on cryptocurrencies are crucial because of the consistency with which ideas are presented. You will learn about the concept of "Airdrops." Airdrops are a recent idea and addition to the cryptocurrency movement. Now, if you aren't reading nor learning more about cryptos, how will you know about this concept and how will you learn how to use it to your advantage?

5.   Volatility

Cryptocurrencies are highly volatile! It is a known fact that digital coins haven't achieved a perfect state of stability thus it is one of the most crucial reasons why you should learn more about this idea. The volatile nature of crypto coins can lead to market changes as well.

A person who is well-informed will know the best times to sell, buy or invest. Yes, they may be affected by the volatile nature of the market, but they will have the upper hand eventually because they've got something that empowers them; it's called knowledge!

6.   Gives you an edge

Earlier on, I asked you about the kind of investor you will want to be and the reason for that question is quite simple. An investor who knows a lot will always have the edge over others who do not know as much as he does. Be a wise investor today by taking the right steps towards solidifying that you identify with advanced lessons. There are more books like this one out there that can add so much value to your experience with cryptos. Buying and reading such materials is an investment in the future that will yield positive results.

With what you've got above, it is quite clear that learning about cryptocurrency from an advanced perspective is crucial. There are ideas you may be conversant with, but you can only become excellent at them when you know more than the basics. Cryptocurrencies can be complicated for a lot of individuals and some people throw in the towel after a few tries as well. If you want to stay motivated, if you're going to be the one who gets to invest with so much enthusiasm then what you should do often is learn, and then learn some more. The next chapter considers the concept of Airdrops and how it relates to cryptocurrencies, head over there now!

George Samaris

Chapter Two

All about Airdrops

With the greater understanding on why you need to learn more about cryptocurrencies at an advanced level, we can proceed to some of the ways through which you can make money using crypto coins. In the world of digital currencies today, there are multiple ways through which you can make money off crypto coins, but not all of them are genuine, if you aren't careful, you might end up losing money. However, Airdrops are one of the most secure ways through which you can make money using cryptocurrencies. If you are still wondering what Airdrops mean, you don't have to worry too much now as in this chapter; we will discuss everything about the concept.

An airdrop for a crypto coin is the process of distributing new tokens by giving them in particular proportions to existing holders of a currency such as Ethereum or Bitcoin. If you hold a type of coin, for instance, you are eligible to take other coins because you are holding the parenting coin through which the Airdrop is done. This method of coin distribution is known as free droppings.

Simply put airdrops mean free coins waiting to be used. The strategy behind the idea is hinged on marketing such that there is increasing awareness for coins to potential investors and crypto users. Today, airdrops have become a very viable tool that suits both the creators of crypto coins and investors; it is a win-win situation as the investors get free coins and the coins receive a significant marketing boost.

There are several reasons why crypto airdrops occur, and one of such purpose is to ensure the even distribution of tokens, so there are no issues around centralization or a particular set of people holding on to a large sum of coins for themselves. Another reason airdrops happen is to reward early investors; a lot of cryptocurrencies want to reward early investors who buy their ICOs or tokens. So the best way to pay them is by giving them more tokens for free. As such, investors are encouraged to buy into particular crypto coins early enough.

Airdrops also happen when there is a new cryptocurrency in the market. What better way to show the world that your crypto creation is the next best thing other than through free distribution? For just spreading awareness on the new coin, holders of popular cryptos (Bitcoin, ethereum, etc.) experience airdrops. Some airdrops take place also to aid marketing and hype for a new coin.

Things needed to participate in airdrops

1.   Ethereum wallet

You will need a wallet that isn't on an exchange, and it should be a personal address that will be compatible with the coins. The private address should most likely be ERC20; this address is mostly compatible with tokens that are airdropped. Yes, the Ethereum wallet must be active; it must show some activity in recent times. Most airdrops check the account the tokens are sent to as a way to ascertain that the recipient didn't create the account for airdrops alone. Now if your wallet isn't active, it will not be able to receive the airdrop.

2.   Telegram account

Because airdrops are mostly a marketing strategy, they rely on platforms that have the number of people they need to boost awareness and telegram is one of such. Some airdrop token requires you to set up a telegram account, and it is advisable that until you receive your coin, you shouldn't delete the telegram account.

3.   An email address

Sometimes airdrops request for an email address, and you can create a spam email if you are not comfortable giving them your email address. However, you should be able to input the password at any time because you might be asked to confirm your email address.

4.   Twitter account

A lot of airdrop accounts will require that you follow them on twitter and even retweet their tweets on the airdrops. The reason they chose twitter is the same as why they decided on telegram; to connect with a more significant number of people.

The fact that airdrops are the perfect gifts makes it much more vulnerable and susceptible to scams and fraudulent activities, but there are steps you can take towards protecting yourself from such issues.

Tips on how to avoid being scammed

1. Don't send monies to addresses

Airdrops are free, and you will never be asked to send money to any address. If you do receive a notification for money to be sent somewhere, immediately steer clear of such an airdrop.

2. Check official and trusted sources

If a particular coin is doing an airdrop, they will most likely announce it on their official website or social media accounts (in most cases Twitter). Always check to confirm from such sites before you decide to participate else you will become a scam victim.

3. Do not send private keys

While dealing with airdrops, you don't have to carry your private keys to anyone for them to check your balance. Your private keys are for your personal use as such, and they should be guarded even from free coins.

As an investor, you might log into your wallet and suddenly see free coins there then it means an airdrop has happened. While it is cool for you to be excited about the freebies, try not to get carried away in the frenzy and misuse the coins. Your first response to an airdrop should be to discover ways through which you can invest the coins. Now, most airdropped coins can only be handy when you invest back in projects that are operated by the currency responsible for the airdrop.

Strategies and concepts like airdrops are some of the reasons why you need to take on advanced lessons on cryptocurrencies. Years ago, there was nothing like an airdrop and years to come; there will be more novel concepts as well; you can only get the best out of them when you read and expand your knowledge base. The next section takes you into the world of cryptocurrency trading platforms; enjoy the read.

Chapter Three

Top ten cryptocurrency trading platforms

With the prices of cryptocurrencies getting better this year, a lot of investors are paying close attention to how they can get more out of digital currencies. There are options when considering trading with cryptos, and one of the most prominent of these options is to utilize the exchanges that make it possible for traders to use fiat currencies (Dollar, Pound, etc.)

Exchanges are a vital part of the cryptocurrency journey, most investors realize how important this is, and that is why they are so keen on using the best cryptocurrency exchanges available in the market. Below, you will find the top ten exchanges currently in the cryptocurrency market.

Top ten Cryptocurrency Exchanges.

1. Binance

This is a Hong Kong-based exchange that is known for charging meager fees (0.1% per trade). The platform accepts and supports quite a number of coins and provides services in several languages including Spanish, Korean, Japanese, Russia, English, and others. During an ICO event, the Binance token known as BNB was created; its primary aim is to fund the development of the exchange.

2. eToro

eToro is a social trading brokerage that has offices in the UK, Cyprus, and Israel. This exchange has got a wide reach across several regulated markets. There are over four million users on the transaction; users can trade in Forex, Stock CFDs and crypto coins as well. eToro set up an OpenBook as well in 2010 that makes it possible for traders to follow, view and replicate the trades of top investors.

3. IQ Option

This platform is a fast-growing one that may be relatively unknown in the broader market yet promises to compete with the big ones as time goes on. There is an opportunity for users to trade in all the popular options with 25% leverage. In addition to these impressive features, the platform gives users a multi-chart layout and technical analysis across all platforms.

4. Coinmama

This exchange is located in Israel and deals primarily in the purchase of Bitcoin with credit cards. Their services are offered in most places around the world, and the buying limits set by the exchange are higher than others. The Bitcoin can be bought using cash or via Western Union making it very easy for investors to take the plunge.

5. Cex.io

This is a Bitcoin exchange that makes it possible for users to buy currencies at meager fees and with the credit card too. Cex.io's services are also available in a lot of countries, and the platform offers four levels that have different buying limits. With this buying limit, investors will be able to know when they need to sell and when they will want to hold on to the coin.

6. Coinbase

If you are trading with cryptocurrency for the first time, then this exchange will be ideal for you. With a user-friendly interface, it is easier for anyone to buy Bitcoin,

Litecoin or Ethereum although most cryptos have to be purchased using Bitcoin. Coinbase makes it possible for users from other countries such as Canada, Uk, Europe, USA to buy Bitcoin utilizing a bank account or credit card.

7. InstaForex

Created in 2007, this exchange has more than seven million users. The exchange also provides support in more than 27 languages and new users, as well as experts, can use the exchange. As a client, you can trade Forex, precious metals, equity indices, and cryptocurrencies.

8. Avatrade

It is effortless for you to open an account with this exchange and within minutes of opening it, you can be trading. If you are not conversant with trading, you will get access to educational materials that will strengthen your knowledge base and help you invest wisely. You can use over 250 trading instruments that include fiat currency, cryptocurrencies, bonds, and CFDs. Another striking feature of this exchange is that it creates a customized trading solution for clients regardless of what they knew before they started using the exchange; it is an enriching experience with this exchange.

9. Youbit.net

Founded in Russia and introduced in 2015, this exchange ensures that Russian, English and Chinese traders can go about trading with so much ease. Youbit.net is a Bitcoin exchange that accepts payment in fiat currency (USD). So if you want to buy Bitcoins, you have to first transfer funds in USD to your account, and then you will be able to trade with Bitcoin, Ethereum, Dash, etc. If you are new to cryptocurrency trades, you will find it very easy to navigate through this site.

10. CRYPTOPIA

This is fast becoming a very popular name in the crypto market. You get to have a free wallet as well as lots of features for trading cryptos such as Bitcoin and Ethereum. You can trade on this exchange for as low as 0.20% of the total amount of Bitcoin or cryptocurrency traded with.

Please note that the top exchanges in the world are not static; they change with time because of the unstable nature of the cryptocurrency market. However, if you are considering investing this year and you will need the best exchanges to work with then you should try out the exchanges listed above.

Investors cannot do without exchanges as such the kind of exchange you use should be a significant concern to you. You are not just looking out for favourite exchanges but for exchanges that function excellently, exchanges that are safe and reliable as well. Now that you know the exchanges to use let's take things up a notch in the next chapter by considering the steps you can take towards trading on an exchange.

*The list contained in this chapter represents the top ten exchanges in the world as at September 2018.

Chapter Four

Steps on how to trade in exchanges

The knowledge you've got now on the types of trading platforms in the market can only become useful when you utilize it through practice. You can practice by actually trading with cryptocurrencies in exchanges this chapter will take you through the most straightforward steps through which you can trade in exchanges and make the most out of your crypto experience.

Step One: Creating an exchange account

The first step to take is to purchase cryptos using fiat money. Now, depending on the exchange you chose, you might be able to own lots of coins using fiat currency. We will use Coinbase as an example of how you can set up your account.

First, you need to create the account by going to coinbase.com after getting your email confirmation; you will be redirected back to Coinbase. Next, you will have to verify your account by using a mobile number; some other exchanges might verify using a Google authenticator. Adding a payment method is very crucial, with Coinbase, you can buy using a debit or credit card, unlike other exchanges that do not allow this. Next, click on "Buy and Sell" on the menu.

When you've got funds in your account, you will be ready to buy your cryptocurrencies; you can choose between Bitcoin, Bitcoin Cash, Litecoin or Ethereum. If you decide to buy and hold the coin, you could stop at this stage. However, if you want to purchase other crypto coins, then you need to follow through with the steps below.

Step Two: Setting up a secondary account

You will need to create a Binance account next, and when you achieve this, you will be able to transfer coins from exchange to exchange.

Step Three: Transfer from exchange to exchange

So why do we want to trade from Binance? Because Binance platform allows you to purchase in four markets (Bitcoin, Ethereum, USDT, and BNB). Next, you will have to click on "Funds" and then on "Deposits," search for Ethereum, you will find a "Deposit" option on the right, click on it and go to the wallet. Make sure you are now at the Ethereum wallet; you will spot your public address where you will make deposits into. Now back to Coinbase, go to your account, select the option "Send" under Ethereum and paste that address you copied from Binance. Check to confirm that the wallet address is correct before you click on send. Because once the funds are sent, you wouldn't get them back. Complete the transfer to the Binance account and wait for a while, so the transfer is confirmed. Try not to send a large sum at first, go for a small amount and if it is successful; you can repeat the process.

Step Four: Make your first crypto trade

Now with money transfer done, it is time to make your early trade. Go back to Binance, select basic or advanced. You will get to see a list of coins, select the coin you want to purchase and click on "Buy." There are other concerns you may want to handle such as using the "Limit order" feature that specifies the exact amount you want to buy. The "Market" option allows you to buy or sell at the current market rate. While "Stop-Limit" places conditional buy/sell orders at a particular price once it gets to an amount you specify.

Knowing how to trade isn't enough for any investor who is keen on making progress with their investment. You've also got to understand the times and seasons of the cryptocurrency markets such that you know the exact time to buy and the time to sell. Aside from traditional buying and selling, you can sell cryptocurrency for cash.

However, not all exchanges trade crypto for cash as most of them only trade crypto-to-crypto. With exchange such as Coinbase, you will be able to trade cryptocurrency for cash. So the central focus for anyone should be to seek out exchanges that allow the use of cash just in case you need to complete a transaction using cash. Although there is a caveat; some exchanges might not have your country's local currency listed as such you will find it difficult trading with cash if you aren't using Dollars, Pounds or any other popularly accepted currency.

Trading with cryptocurrency is akin to being on a rollercoaster ride.you will have perfect moments, and then you will also have challenging moments that make you wish you never got on this journey in the first place but in all, it will be worth it. Cryptocurrencies are not an easy venture to get involved with, but if you are an investor who loves to take risks and enjoys the thrills of winning, you will most likely have a lot of fun.

As an investor, trading with cryptocurrency will be a part of your daily experience. At first, you might make a mistake which is why it is advised that you trade with small amounts first before going all the way with the significant funds. The more you trade, the better you become and the more experience you garner. So buy coins today, buy some and keep for a while till the market stabilizes, buy coins and trade, buy to invest, to gift to others, etc. Your portfolio as an investor wouldn't grow until you do something about it; you can take that step today. Above all don't trade with cryptocurrencies thinking you will never make a hit in the form of a loss; losses are a vital part of the learning and building process. It may hurt, but it will help you grow as an investor long term.

Chapter Five

Support and resistance with cryptocurrencies

The fact that you are reading this material on advanced cryptocurrency is a sign that you are already involved with cryptos, but you may be struggling with the volatile nature of the currencies and wondering how you can deal with it. What you need to do is learn how to identify support and resistance levels. Support can be defined as a level where the price of an asset drops with more buyers willing to buy it at that low level thus leading to an increase in demand. The increase in demand as the price goes down creates "Support."

"Resistance" on the other hand is a price level that entails a pause due to sales at that price level. You can determine support and resistance in various ways such as backtesting which entails considering the historical movement of price to ascertain where the price falters. If an asset is overvalued at a price level, sellers will take advantage of such as asset.

Think of support like a temporary floor or a haven for investors who are seeking the easiest way to get into the market. The pressure from so many people to buy prevents the price from falling any further. When there is increased pressure to buy a particular thing, the level of concentration increases thus forcing the price to act as a barrier but with resistance the price level will be at the ceiling and not on the floor (Support).

It is possible for support to become resistance especially if the price falls below resistance levels. If a particular price falls below its support line, then the demand for the specific asset was not be strong enough to hold on to the support. Traders know that certain price levels make it difficult for them to push the price an asset in a particular direction. So let's say we have a MR. X who observes that the amount can't just get above $49 for over many months even though it gets close to it. Now traders will refer to that price as the resistance level because it is preventing the market from moving the price upwards.

So what is the implication of support and resistance for investors like Mr. X?

1.   Helps investors determine the future

Well, for starters, investors will be able to determine future resistance and support levels thus aiding their returns on investments. Knowledge of resistance and support also make it possible for investors to strategize effectively in a way that suits their plans for the future.

2.   Making trade decisions

Major trade decisions will be hinged on the level of understanding the investor has about support and resistance. When it comes to cryptocurrency, there are a lot of things to consider especially with pricing because if a mistake is made and the funds are already transferred it will be difficult for the investor to get the money back. More so, whatever trade decisions an investor wants to take, he/she will always check the support and resistance level to get

3. Affects the volume at price levels

The more buying and selling has taken place at a particular level, the more the resistance level will be. Traders and investors always remember these prices and are quick to use them. However, when there are activities under high volume, the price will drop and at that stage, there will only be transactions when the rate is stable again. Investors will prefer to trade at a breakeven point than trade at a loss.

With advanced cryptocurrency lessons, there are a whole lot more to learn other than how to buy and sell cryptocurrencies. There are technical terms every investor must understand for them to take advantage of the times and seasons in the crypto market. Support and resistance are examples of such terms and if you can grasp exactly what they mean, they will affect your investment plans positively.

Another term you should also become conversant with is the idea behind day trading; the next chapter is replete with information on how you can use this concept as an investor who is passionate about making progress with cryptocurrencies.

Chapter Six

The concept of Day trading

Our last idea is going to be all about the concept of Day Trading.

There are multiple trading strategies out there from individuals who are not investors, as much as you seek after knowledge and how to grow your investments, you must always also be mindful of whom you listen to and the kind of advice you adopt. I have tried Day Trading multiple times and can say that it is the strategy you should try out if you are going to take your cryptocurrency investment seriously.

So, I have been able to make the steady profit off the cryptocurrency market, the successes and profit came to fruition as a result of me trying and failing multiple times while learning vital lessons in the process. So what is Day Trading? Day Trading is one of the fastest means through which profit can be made while selling cryptos. It entails the speculation of prices of the currencies while buying and selling within a day to get a profit. Day Trading as a term was derived from traditional stocks that required a very fast "In and out" trading by the hour.

Think of Day Trading as you going to the farmers market with the produce from your farm. You get to the market, and within a particular period, you can sell off your products and make a lot of profit all in one day. However, with Day Trading, you should know that the same way you've got the potential to make money is the same way you can lose money. I will share some fundamentals about Day Trading with you below; these fundamentals will provide more insight into what the strategy is about.

The fundamentals include;

1. Define your goal before trading

Before you start trading with cryptos using the Day trading strategy, you need to make sure you've got a definite objective. The cryptocurrency market isn't a stable one, you may lose money in the long term, but if you know precisely why you are trading, you will become conscious of what you are doing to achieve that goal. Now when you fulfil that objective, you don't have to hold on to the coins again.

2.   Be mindful of exchange fees

When you trade multiple times over a period, it could accumulate trading fees that are charged by the exchanges. You can avoid this by placing a one buy, and one sell order so if you post this and someone accepts your price, the deal is complete. However, if you take the process of someone else (when it is listed in another book), you will have to pay a higher exchange fee to the exchange. Always check the structure of the exchange you are trading with so you don't lose money to the exchanges.

3.   Do not buy a coin for Fear of Missing out

Please, do not buy coins when you are under pressure. For example, you might complete an excellent trade and then after you see the coin's value increases. Investors try to buy back the coin because of the fear of missing out on the profit, but this is the quickest way to lose money. If the coin fluctuates that same day again, you will lose all the money you put in back.

4.   Use limit orders

This step helps you create a stop loss order after you buy a coin on a particular trade. What you do here is quite simple; you have to set a specific price at which you will exit the business should the coin drop below a certain point. So if the price falls lower than the price you've set, the exchange sells the coin at the price you set thus helping you minimize loss.

5.   Get the breakfast of resistance

We talked about resistance in a previous chapter, and this is a strategy that will help you when trading. Resistance refers to the level at which the price of a coin would not break through without dropping back to a lower level known as support. When there is a breakout, you should think about buying the currency at that point. You can set off trading alerts as well, so you are notified about breakouts thus helping you scale through with a profit quickly.

The cryptocurrency market is quite volatile, and it explains the reason why Day Trading might be a challenge for beginners. However, you need to start building your portfolio, and it begins with taking risks, trying new things and investing more often even if it leads to mistakes. This brings us to the end of a fantastic chapter and also the end of this book; there is a special message embedded in the next section for you, head over there to discover the news and more.

George Samaris

Chapter Seven

Altcoin Ninjas; the path way to winning cryptocurrency trading

The team at Altcoin Ninjas recognize that a lot of people have questions about trading, buying and investing with cryptocurrencies hence they are online 24 hours of the day ready to take your questions and enquiries.

This organization was set up for you, they are functioning and working excellently because of you so what will you rather do? You can take advantage of what they offer by becoming a ninja who always on top with all things crypto coins. There are various ways through which you can engage this organization and this just makes it so exciting. As opposed to just having a number to call and talk on, you can actually join the community online and gain access to multiple resources and top-notch personnel that can bridge the gap between you and all the money you can make with crypto coins.

One of the most striking features of the Altcoin Ninjas organization is the fact that the group isn't just focused on the ways to sell and trade crypto coins. Oh, there is so much more to what they can do for you and one of the numerous services they offer is the sale of unique and effective tools that will aid your trading experience. You will be able to trade in style and comfort with the myriad of tools, materials and equipment offered on the site. Now you can say "goodbye" to the days of trading in discomfort and not knowing the right tools to purchase.

From classy and comfortable chairs to monitors, trading tools, mining equipment and a host of other merchandise. The Altcoin Ninja is your one stop site for information and inventory how cool is that? There is so much more you can enjoy with this group and that includes buying Bitcoin at a 5-8 discount rate than you can find on exchanges, you will be certain of buying real Bitcoins without stress and even getting them at a discounted rate. No scam stories and no delays. You do have the option to become a Samurai or a Sensai; more information on this is on the site. Visit www.altninjas.com and get ready to burst into the world of possibilities with crypto coins.

The world has embraced the concept of social media more than ever before. Now people connect with one another all over the world via social media and who says you cannot do the same with crypto coins? Altcoin Ninjas is active on so many social media platforms; Facebook, Twitter, Instagram, LinkedIn and Pinterest. You can also watch enlightening videos and inspiring content that propels you to make better decisions via YouTube. When you subscribe, you join a movement of people who are passionate about making a difference in their finances with cryptocurrencies and knowing how to go about it the right way.

Altcoin Ninjas organization is more than a site, I can tell you that it is a community that thrives on lifting one another up. There are ninja benefits you enjoy as a member, you just sign up and enter the arena of good vibes and great investment opportunities. Leave the job of carrying out research on ICOs to the Altcoin Ninjas organization, you will also get to know the ICOs they will be investing in thus creating a clear path for you to follow. If you still like there are more questions and concerns bothering you then take a break from chatting with reps and speak directly with the CEO, oh wow! You see, Altcoin Ninjas is strategically positioned to help you become the best version of yourself and also help you get ahead with your cryptocurrency journey.

The reason there is panic within some people with respect to cryptocurrencies is because they have heard of how others make mistakes with their cryptos. Some people who have decided not to invest in crypto coins make their decision based on a lack of understanding of key concepts. However, all of these can be laid to rest when you have a solid team backing you up and providing you with the best services. Altcoin Ninjas was founded on the principle of making life generally easier for its subscribers. We know that money affects the quality of life people live; good money decisions means living well and enjoying life. So, we are dedicated to helping individuals take advantage of the good opportunities crypto coins offer to make their lives better than it is now.

Conclusion

The quest to demystify cryptocurrency is one that entails a lot of reading, learning, unlearning and relearning. It is not a one-way path that leads to a final destination; it is a series of roads on a roadmap that leads to various channels that are interconnected. What we have achieved with this book is to help the reader have a firm grasp of what it means to be a crypto investor.

We embarked on this journey together getting acquainted with the reasons why we should continue in the next chapter. Right after that, the concept of Airdrops was presented. Trading platforms and how to trade successfully were also considered as well as the idea of support and resistance. We rounded off with Day trading, and i believe you have learned so much from the sections and chapters we have in this book.

My previous book on cryptocurrencies did so well in the market, and it inspired me to take my readers on another journey that will make them become better investors. Everything you have read thus far is subject to change shortly; it is, this is because cryptocurrencies are ever evolving. So, you may ask; does this mean i have to read more books in the future continually? Oh yes, it most certainly means that!

Thank you for being such a good sport and reading with me till this point. You have shown dedication and passion; there is a reward for it; your prize is increased awareness of how cryptos work and the best investments that will be profitable for you in the future. Thank you for taking the time to read, please feel free to share your thoughts and success stories with me; it will be fun to learn about the impact this book has on you and your financial journey as well. Best wishes to you on this venture.